THE ARTS OF PERSIA &
OTHER COUNTRIES OF ISLAM

LECTOR HOUSE PUBLIC DOMAIN WORKS

THE ARTS OF PERSIA &
OTHER COUNTRIES OF ISLAM

HAGOP KEVORKIAN

ISBN: 978-93-89956-23-8

Published: 1926

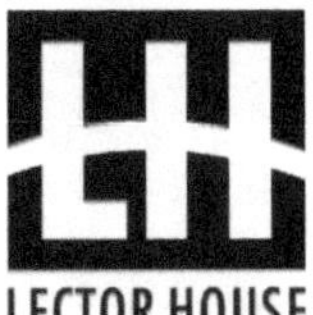

LECTOR HOUSE LLP
E-MAIL: lectorpublishing@gmail.com

SPECIAL EXHIBITION

THE ARTS OF PERSIA &
OTHER COUNTRIES OF ISLAM

BY

H. KEVORKIAN COLLECTION

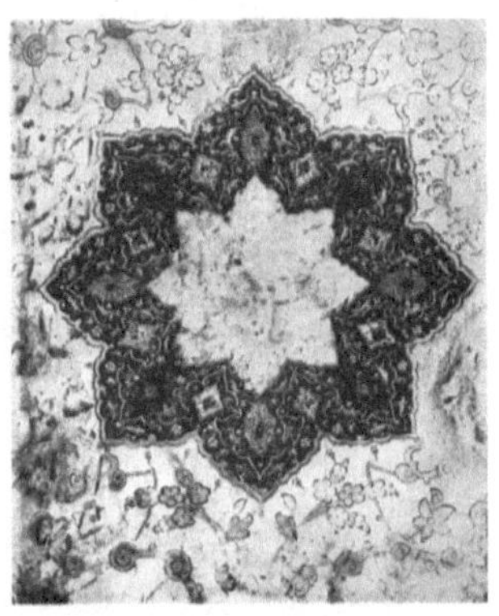

**FROM THURSDAY, APRIL TWENTY-SECOND TO
SATURDAY, MAY FIFTEENTH, INCLUSIVE
ON THE ENTIRE THIRD FLOOR**

1926

THE ARTS OF PERSIA &
OTHER COUNTRIES OF ISLAM

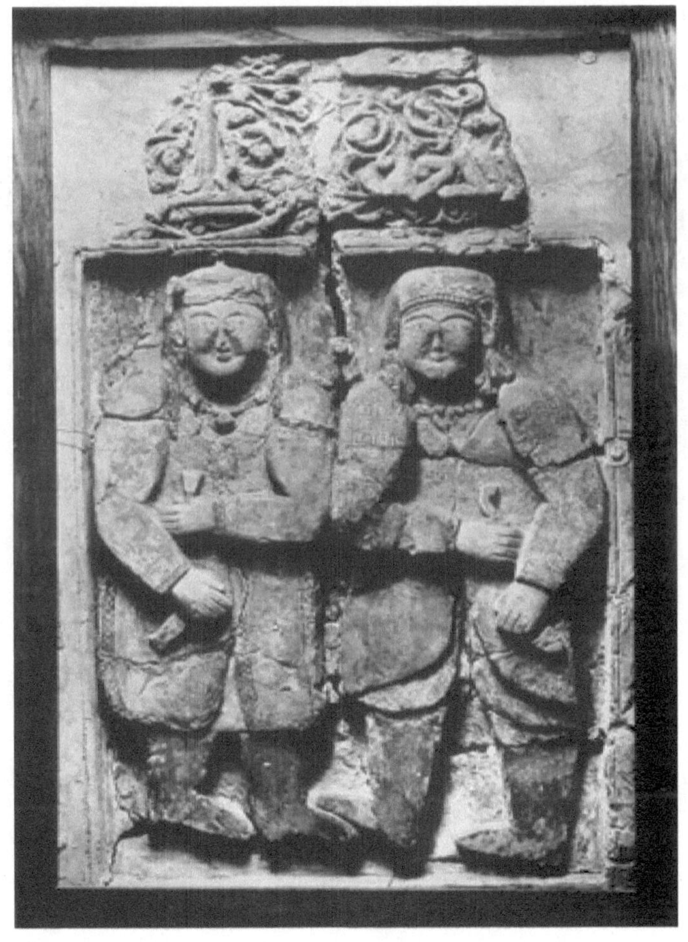

STUCCO BAS-RELIEF, PAINTED IN POLYCHROME. EXCAVATED
AT RAY (RHAGES) ANTERIOR TO THE XIITH CENTURY

THIS exhibition has been arranged with a desire to meet the convenience of those who are interested in manifestations of the arts of different countries over which Islam held sway at one time or other in the past. An effort has been made to show under one roof representative examples of works produced at different epochs and stages of the civilizations referred to, so that they may be seen, and perhaps studied, with the minimum expenditure of time.

Fine examples of many branches of the arts of these peoples are in permanent exhibitions at the Metropolitan Museum, New York, and the museums of great cities throughout the country. It is difficult to find adequate words to describe the enchanting atmosphere of the halls at the Metropolitan Museum where Near Eastern art is installed; and the same can truly be said of the Museum of Fine Arts, Boston, and the University of Pennsylvania Museum, Philadelphia. These exhibitions must inevitably contribute to the enjoyment and education of countless visitors to these institutions, and will continue to do so in increasing degree to the enjoyment of generations to come.

The present exhibition does not comprise a vast number of objects. Its claim to attention lies in the fact that it includes an important series of really first class works which are also of great historical importance. There will be on view as well some comparatively new types of objects of æsthetic and archæological interest, obtained as the result of recent excavations.

The briefness of time available precluded the possibility of compiling a catalogue, as was at first intended. The present booklet is issued to explain the scope of the exhibition, and extend a cordial invitation to visit it.

H.K.

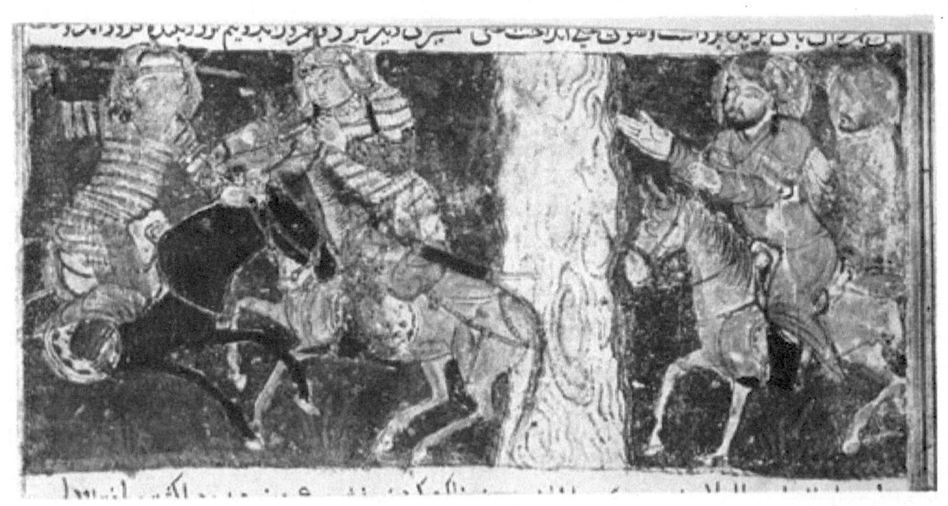

MUHAMMAD (THE PROPHET) WITNESSES ALI (HIS SON-IN-LAW AND SUCCESSOR) DEFEAT AMR BEN ABDWAD

One of the eight illustrations for a XIIIth Century Persian Manuscript entitled, "HISTORY OF TABARI", compiled A.H. 310 (A.D. 922). The present copy is a subsequent one of the Persian version, translated by AL B'ALA'MI, A.H. 352.

It is interesting to note that TABARI records in the book here referred to, that three messages were sent by MUHAMMAD to KHUSRAW PARNIZ, imparting the divine warnings. One of the messages, as recorded in an old Manuscript entitled NIHAYAT UL-IRAB, reads:

"In the name of God, the merciful, the compassionate. From MUHAMMAD the Apostle of God to KHUSRAW son of HURMAZD. But to proceed. Verily I extol unto thee God, beside whom there is no other God. He it is who guarded me when I was an orphan, and made me rich when I was destitute, and guided me when I was straying in error. Only he who is bereft of understanding, and over whom calamity triumphs, rejects the message which I am sent to announce. O KHUSRAW, submit and thou shalt be safe, or else prepare to wage with God and with his Apostle a war which shall not find them helpless. Farewell."

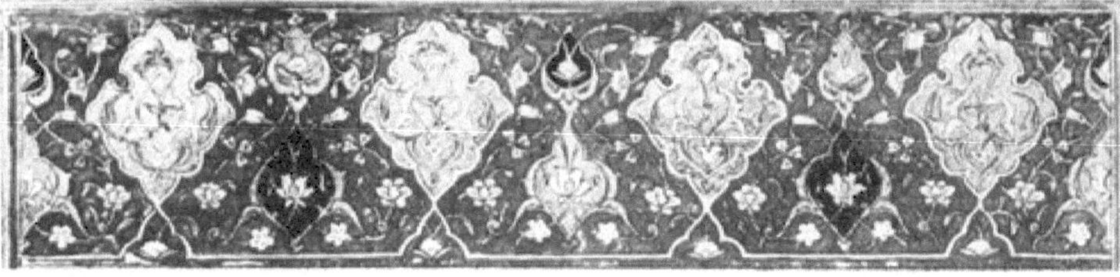

The rise of ISLAM and its rapid advent to power, is perhaps the most surprising chapter of the history of mankind. The great empires, Persian and Byzantine, which were subjected to the urgent onslaught of this rising power may have been in an enfeebled condition as a result of excess of despotism and internal dissensions, as historians affirm; but that the element of the power must have been in the rationality of the principles contained in the teaching, there can be no doubt.

"It was undoubtedly to ISLAM, that simple yet majestic creed of which no unprejudiced student can ignore the grandeur, that Arabs owed the splendid part which they were destined to play in the history of civilization. In judging of the Arabian Prophet, western critics are too often inclined to ignore the condition from which he raised his country, and to forget that many institutions which they condemn were not introduced but only tolerated by ISLAM. The early Muslims were very sensible of the immense amelioration in their life effected by MUHAMMAD's teachings. What this same amelioration was is well shown in the following passage from the oldest extant biography of the Prophet," says Professor G. Browne in his memorable work on Persia,[1] and quotes IBN HISHAM (A.H. 213: A.D. 828) in support.

"During the first half of the seventh century," says DOZY in his excellent work on ISLAM,[2] "everything followed its accustomed course in the Byzantine as in the Persian Empire. These two states continued always to dispute the possession of western Asia; they were, to all outward appearance, flourishing; the taxes which poured into the treasuries of their Kings reached considerable sums, and the magnificence, as well as the luxury of their capitals had become proverbial. But all this was but in appearance, for secret disease consumed both empires; they were burdened by a crushing despotism; on either hand the history of the dynasties formed a concatenation of horrors, that of the state a series of persecutions born of dissensions in religious matters. At this juncture it was that, all of a sudden, there emerged from deserts hardly known and appeared on the scene of the world a new people, hitherto divided into innumerable nomad tribes, who, for the most part, had been at war with one another, now for the first time united. It was this people, passionately attached to liberty, simple in their food and dress, noble and hospitable, gay and witty, but at the same time proud, irascible, and, once their passions were aroused, vindictive, irreconcilable and cruel, who overthrew in an instant the venerable but rotten empire of the Persians, snatched from the successors of Constantine their fairest provinces, trampled under their feet a Germanic kingdom but lately founded, and menaced the rest of Europe, while at the same time, at the other end of the world, its victorious armies penetrated to the Himalayas. Yet it was not like so many other conquering peoples, for it preached at the same time a new religion. In opposition to the dualism of the Persians and a degenerate Christianity, it announced a pure monotheism which was accepted by millions of men, and which, even in our own time, constitutes the religion of a tenth part of the human race."

---

[1] "Literary History of Persia," by Edward G. Browne, M.A., M.B., Vol. I, page 186.

[2] Translated into French by Victor Chauvin under the title of "Essai sur l'Histoire de l'Islamisme" (Leyden and Paris, 1879).

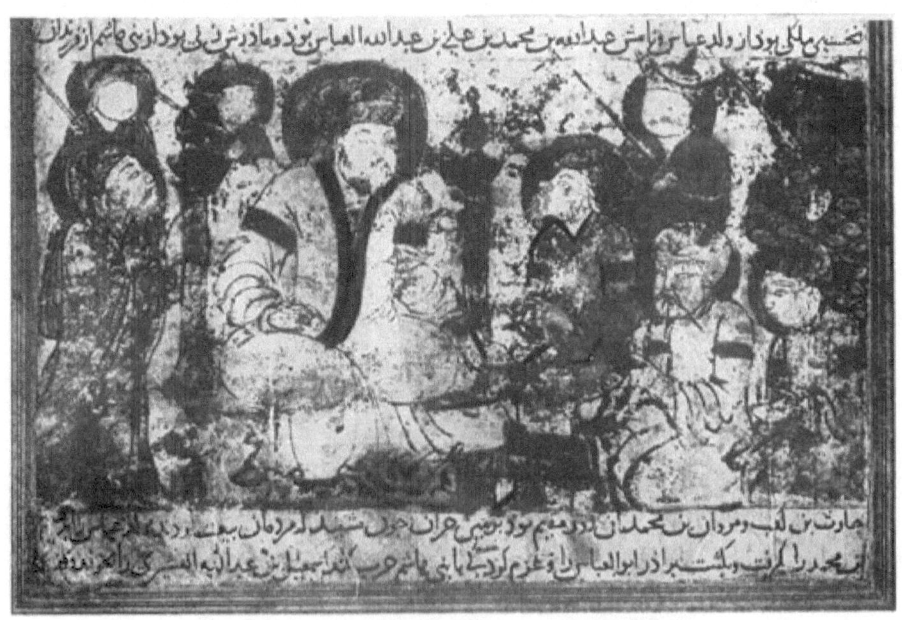

ACCESSION AT KUFA, A.D. 749, OF ABU'L-ABBAS ABDULLAH AS-SAFFAH FIRST CALIPH OF THE HOUSE OF ABBAS

One of eight illustrations for a XIIIth Century Manuscript entitled, "History of Tabari", compiled A.H. 310 (A.D. 922). The present copy is a subsequent one of the Persian version, translated by al B'ala'mi, A.H. 352.

"It was a dynasty abounding in good qualities, richly endowed with generous attributes, wherein the wares of science found a ready sale, the merchandise of culture was in great demand, the observances of religion were respected, charitable bequests flowed freely ... and the frontiers were bravely kept." — Al-Fakhri (historian of fame of the XIIIth Century) on the Abbasid Dynasty.

The teachings of Muhammad were not of a nature to arouse intolerance.[3] History does not record the practice of compulsory conversion in the scheme of conquest of early converts. "It is often supposed," says Professor Browne, "that the choice offered by the warriors of Islam was between the Qur'an and the Sword; this, however, is not the fact." There are innumerable evidences to the contrary

---

[3] "Righteousness is not that ye turn your faces to the East and to the West, but righteousness is this: Whosoever believeth in God, and the last day, and the angels, and the book, and the prophets; and whoso, for the love of God, giveth of his wealth unto his kindred, and unto orphans, and the poor, and the traveller, and to those who crave alms, and for the release of the captives; and whoso observeth prayer and giveth in charity; and those who, when they have covenanted, fulfil their covenant; and who are patient in adversity and hardship, and in times of violence: these are the righteous and they that fear the Lord." — Qur'an, Sura II.

which history records.[4] It appears that the exemplary behavior of the Arabs, under their newly acquired faith, was the main factor not only in the success of their scheme of conquest, but also in the impression which it made on the defeated in determining them to adopt the faith which produced such upright warriors.

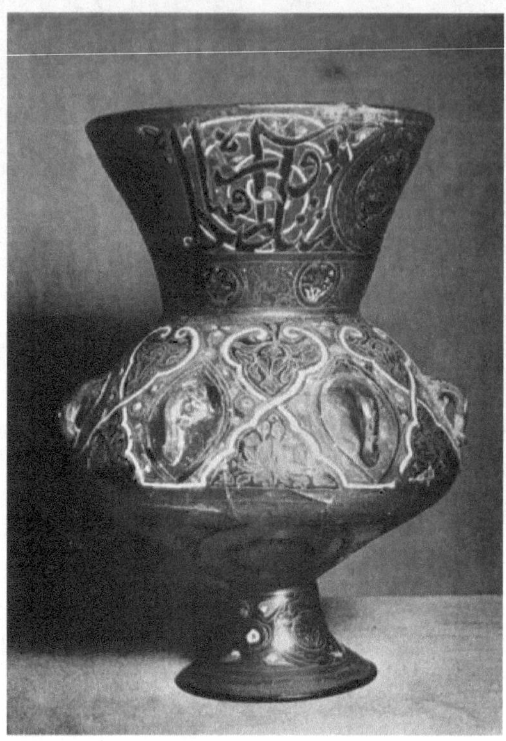

POLYCHROME ENAMELLED GLASS MOSQUE LAMP OF THE XIIITH CENTURY

Very few examples of this highly advanced art survive. They represent an extremely aristocratic manifestation of art and were executed by order of MAMELUKE CALIPHS of Egypt, and dedicated by them to their great Mosques, individually inscribed in magnificent calligraphy.

The tremendous political upheaval that the evolution of ISLAM brought in its train to the affairs of the world does not fall within the scope of this paper. A high-

[4] The treaty concluded by HABIB B. MASLAMA with the people of DABIL in Armenia ran as follows: "In the name of God the merciful, the clement. This is a letter from HABIB B. MASLAMA to the people of DABIL, Christians, Magians, and Jews, such of them as are present and such of them as are absent. Verily I guarantee the safety of your lives, properties, churches, temples and city walls; ye are secure, and it is incumbent upon us faithfully to observe this treaty so long as you observe it and pay the poll-tax and the land-tax. God is witness, and he sufficeth as a witness."—QUR'AN, V. 104. Concerning the acceptance of the Poll-Tax from ZOROASTRIANS, as well as from Jews and Christians. A. VON KREMER's "Kulturgeschichte d. Orients," Vol. I, page 59.

ly important fact, however, must not be lost sight of, that by consolidating and uni-fying the tottering states a new civilization was founded which knew how to turn to account the culture of the ancient states conquered. In this overwhelming trans-formation Persia came in, from the outset, to play the most conspicuous and im-portant part. The artistic productions of the MUHAMMADAN world that have come down to us as living monuments, substantiate this statement without a shadow of doubt, which makes it unnecessary to resort to recorded history, although its pages abound with incontestable evidences.[5]

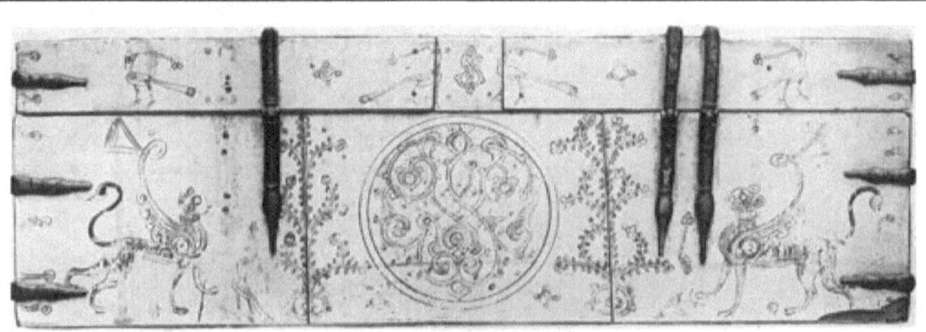

ROYAL IVORY BOX, WITH METAL MOUNTING. HIS-PANO-ARABIAN ART, XIITH-XIIITH CENTURY DECORATED IN ENAMEL AND GOLD, DEPICTING INSIGNIA OF SUCCES-SORS OF UMAYYAD CALIPHS OF SPAIN, AND QUR'ANIC ROSETTES AND KUFIC CALLIGRAPHY OF THE HIGHEST DIS-TINCTION

[5] "Thus it is by no means correct to imply that the two or three centuries immediately following the MUHAMMADAN conquest of Persia were a blank page in the intellectual life of its people. It is, on the contrary, a period of immense and unique interest, of fusion between the old and the new, of transformation of forms and transmigration of ideas, but in no wise of stagnation or death. Politically, it is true, Persia ceased for a while to enjoy a separate national existence, being merged in that great MUHAMMADAN EMPIRE which stretched from GIBRALTAR to the JAXARTES; but in the intellectual domain she soon began to assert the su-premacy to which the ability and subtlety of her people entitled her. Even the forms of State organization were largely adapted from Persian models."—AL-FAKHRI (ed. AHLWARDT, page 101), on the organization of the DIWANS or Government offices.

"In the finance department not only was the Persian system adopted, but the Persian language and notation continued to be used till the time of AL-HAJJAJ B. YUSUF (about A.D. 700)."—EDWARD G. BROWNE, "Literary History of Persia", Vol. I, page 204.

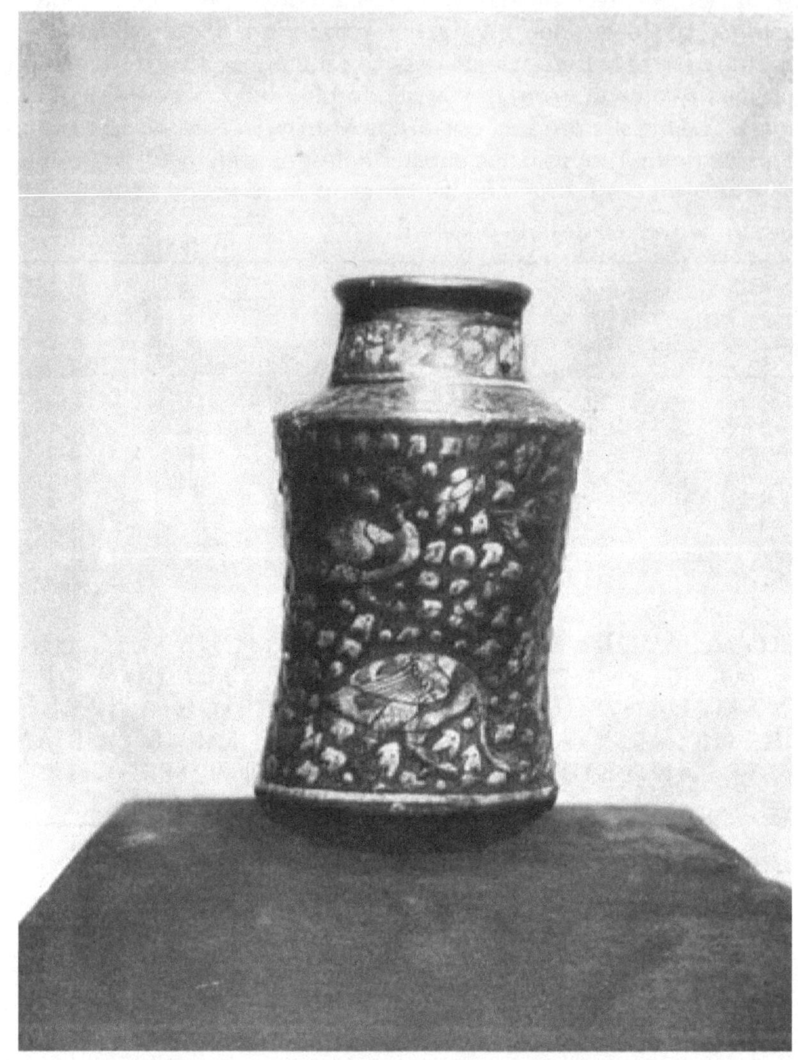

FAIENCE CYLINDRICAL VASE, WITH RELIEF AND LUSTRE DECORATION. FROM FOSTAT (ANCIENT CAIRO), DYNASTY OF FATIMID ANTI-CALIPHS (A.D. 974-1171)

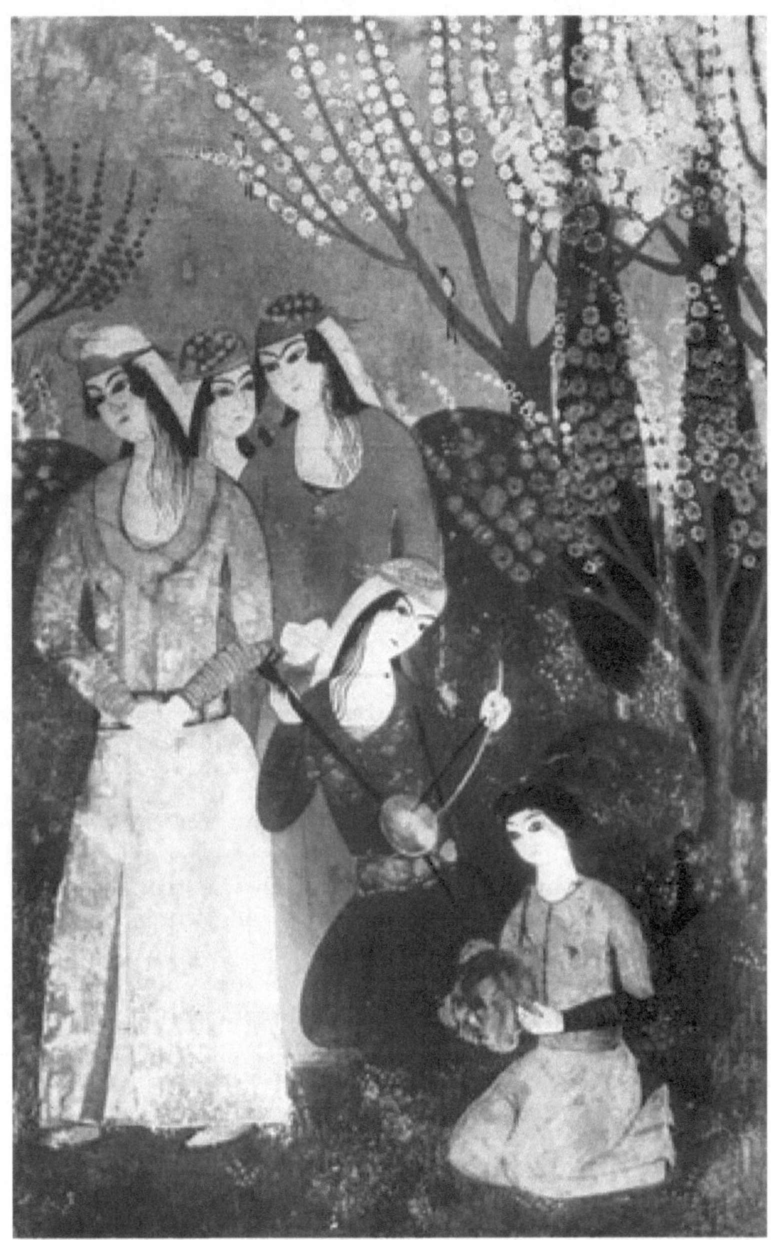

AN EARLY SAFAWID PAINTING (CIRCA A.D. 1525) OF EXQUI-
SITE RHYTHM, DEPTH AND DIGNITY

It would be difficult to offer an explanation for the underlying unity and in-
tegrity of character manifest in the artistic expression of the MUHAMMADAN countries, of vast geographical range, without a clear understanding of the vital force

contained in the teachings of the Arabian Apostle, and the characteristics of his people, destined to carry those teachings from one end of the earth to the other. For this reason the foregoing brief survey has been ventured.

There can be no doubt that the pivot around which the artistic activities of Muhammadan countries revolved, was Persia.[6] She was to attain the function of the Sun, element of her old faith, source of sustaining energy; and continued to radiate into these planets of countries and races of the System, her all-stimulating cultural beams, the reflection of which is discernible in all artistic manifestations of those countries. In the field of literature, which is so little known in the western world, the influence is even greater than in the visual art with which we are concerned. Muhammadan literature, be it Arabic, Turkish, or Persian, is Persian in spirit and feeling.[7]

ILLUSTRATIONS FOR TITLE-PAGES OF A SHAHNAMA (Epic of Kings) of the XVth Century.

Representing Timur-i-Lang (A.H. 736-807) attending a festival. The name and the full titles of Timur appear in excellent Thuluth lettering round the border of the rug upon which the monarch sits.

This important Manuscript was presented by the Emperor of Russia to the Ambassador of Persia at St. Petersburg, A.D. 1829. The Ambassador's autograph inscription reads:

"The Shahnama graciously presented by H.M. the Emperor at my third visit—may it be omen of good fortune. Muhammad Ali ibni Ghafouri Ambassador, 22nd of Rajab, A.H. 1245."

"Timur Beg was seated in a portal, in front of the entrance of a beautiful Palace; and he was sitting on the ground.... The lord was seated cross-legged, on silken embroidered carpets, amongst round pillows. He was dressed in a robe of silk, with white headdress on his head, on the top of which there was a spinel ruby, with pearls and precious stones round it. As soon as the ambassadors saw the lord, they made a reverential bow, placing the knee on the ground, and crossing the arms on the breast; then they went forward and made another and then a third, remaining with their knees on the ground. The lord ordered them to rise and come forward.... Three Mirzas, or secretaries, ... came and took the ambassadors by the arms, and led them forward until they stood before the lord.... He asked after the King, saying, 'How is my son the King? is he in good health?' When the ambassa-

[6] "The ascendancy of the Persians over the Arabs, that is to say of the conquered over the victors, had already for a long while been in course of preparation; it became complete when the Abbasids, who owed their elevation to the Persians, ascended the throne (A.D. 749). The most distinguished personages at court were consequently Persians. The famous Barmecides were descended from a Persian noble who had been superintendent of the Fire Temple at Balkh. Afshin, the all-powerful favorite of the Caliph al-Mutasim, was a scion of the Princes of Usrushna in Transoxiana."—Dozy, "Histoire de l'Islamisme".

[7] "With the rise of Persian influence, there opened an era of culture, toleration, and scientific research. The practice of oral tradition was also giving place to recorded statement and historical narrative,—a change hastened by the scholarly tendencies introduced from the East."—Sir William Muir, on the rise of the Abbasid Dynasty.

dors had answered, Timur Beg turned to the knights who were seated around him, amongst whom were one of the sons of Toktamish, the former Emperor of Tartary, several chiefs of the blood of the late Emperor of Samarquand, and others of the family of the lord himself, and said, 'Behold, here are the ambassadors sent by my son, the King of Spain, who is the greatest King of Franks, and lives at the end of the world. These Franks are truly great people, and I will give my benediction to the King of Spain, my son." — From the Diary of Ruy Gonzalez di Clavijo, principal of the embassy despatched A.D. 1404 to the Court of Samarquand by Henry III of Castile, Spain.

Clavijo describes the beautiful gardens with their tiled palaces where banquets were given. The ambassador, who was invited, marvelled at the gorgeous tents, one of which "was so large and high that from a distance it looked like a castle, and it was a very wonderful thing to see, and possessed more beauty than it is possible to describe". It is interesting to notice that Sharaf-u-din mentions the presence of the Ambassadors, "for," he writes, "even the smallest of fish have their place in the sea". Truly a delightful touch! — History of Persia, by Sir Percy Sykes, Vol. II, page 133.

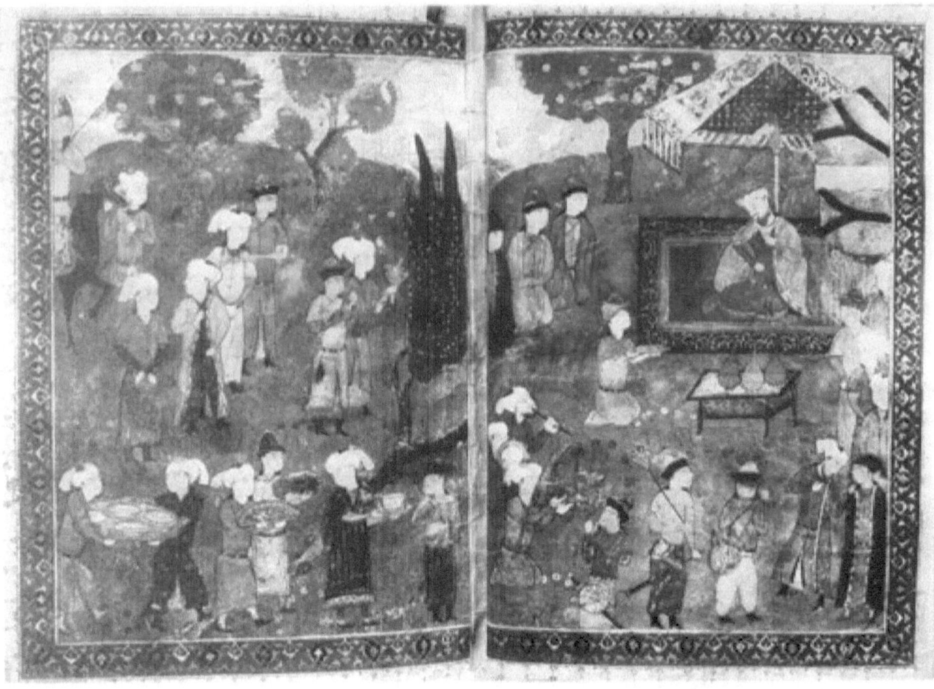

ILLUSTRATIONS FOR TITLE-PAGES OF A SHAHNAMA (EPIC OF KINGS) OF THE XVTH CENTURY

"On the extreme of the western side of the royal precincts opening on to the Chahar Bagh are a garden and building. The Garden was previously called "Bagh i Bulbul" (Garden of Nightingales). — Lord Curzon, History of Persia.

"Night drawing on, all the pride of SPAHAUN was met in the CHAUR BAUG and grandees were airing themselves, prancing about with their numerous trains, striving to outdo each other in pomp and generosity." —DR. FRYER, recorded A.D. 1677.

CHARDIN, who was at Ispahan at the time of SHAH SULEIMAN's reign (1667-1694), records in his "VOYAGES", Vol. VIII, page 43:

"When one walks in these places expressly made for the delights of love and when one passes through all these cabinets and niches, one's heart is melted to such an extent that to speak candidly, one always leaves with a very ill grace. The climate without doubt contributes much towards exciting this amorous disposition, but assuredly these places, although in some respects little more than cardboard castles, are nevertheless more smiling and agreeable than our most sumptuous palaces."

LORD CURZON says (History of Persia, Vol. II, page 37) that "Even CHARDIN, enthusiastic but seldom sentimental, was inspired to an unwonted outburst by the charms of HASHT BAHISHT".

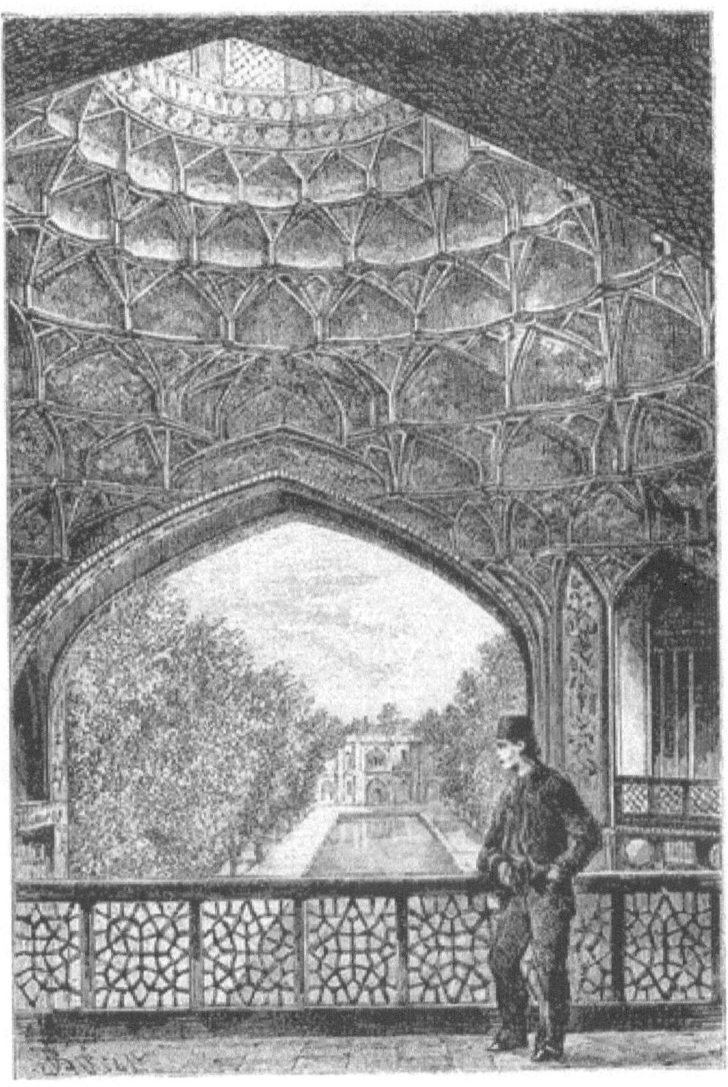

VIEW OF CHAHAR BAGH (FOUR GARDENS) AND HASHT BA-HISHT (PAVILION OF EIGHT PARADISES) AT ISPAHAN. CON-STRUCTED BY SHAH SULEIMAN SAFAWI ABOUT A.D. 1670. RE-PRODUCTION FROM "LA PERSE, LA CHALDEE ET LA SUSIANE" (1887) BY DIEULAFOY

PAIR OF DOORS FROM THE PAVILION OF CHAHAL SITUN (Hall of Forty Pillars) built by SHAH ABBAS the Great (A.D. 1588-1629).

These are decorated with representations of scenes from the Royal Court of the great Shah, painted minutely by Court artists.

"They transport us straight to the Court of the lordly ABBAS and his predecessors or successors on the throne.... We see the King engaged at some royal festivity enjoying the pleasure of the Bowl." —Lord Curzon, History of Persia, Vol. II, page 34.

Ker Porter, who saw the Palace of Chahal Situn in its perfect condition, records: "The exhaustless profusion of its splendid materials reflected not merely their own golden lights on each other, but all the variegated colours of the Garden, so that the whole surface seemed formed of polished silver and mother of pearl set with precious stones."

Lord Curzon, who visited it soon after its last repair in 1891, quotes Ker Porter and by way of contrast says: "The bulk of this superb decoration which still remains in the Throne Room behind, to point bitter contrast, had on the walls of the Loggia been ruthlessly obliterated by the brush of the painter, who had left in its place pink wash; had I caught the Pagan, I would gladly have suffocated him in a barrel of his own paint." —History of Persia, Vol. II, page 33.

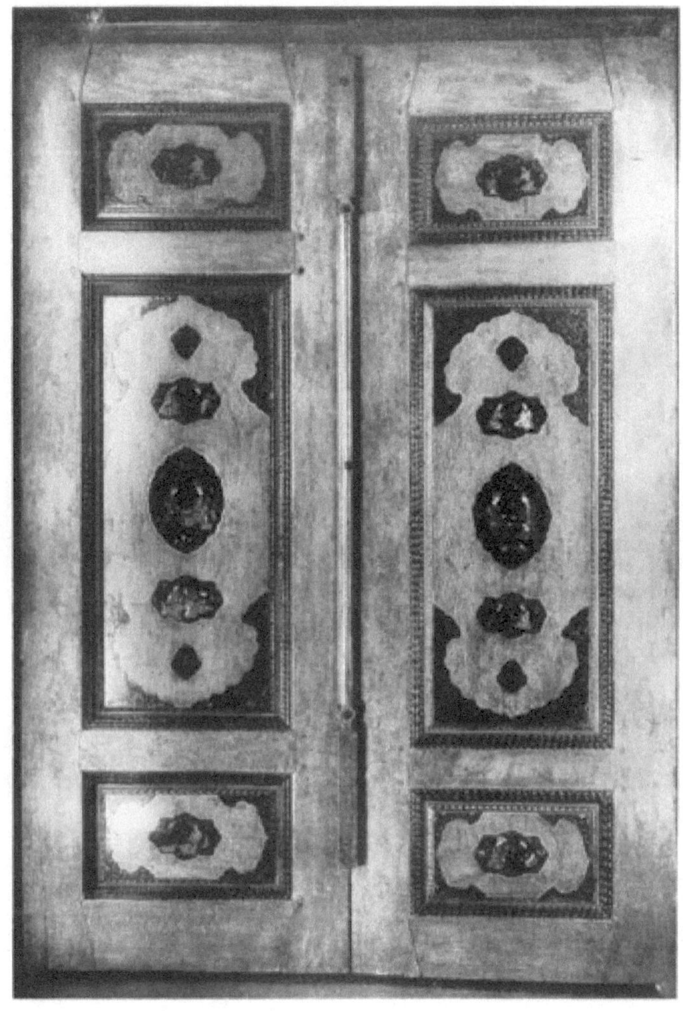

PAIR OF DOORS FROM THE PAVILION OF CHAHAL SITUN
(HALL OF FORTY PILLARS) BUILT BY SHAH ABBAS THE GREAT
(A.D. 1588-1629)

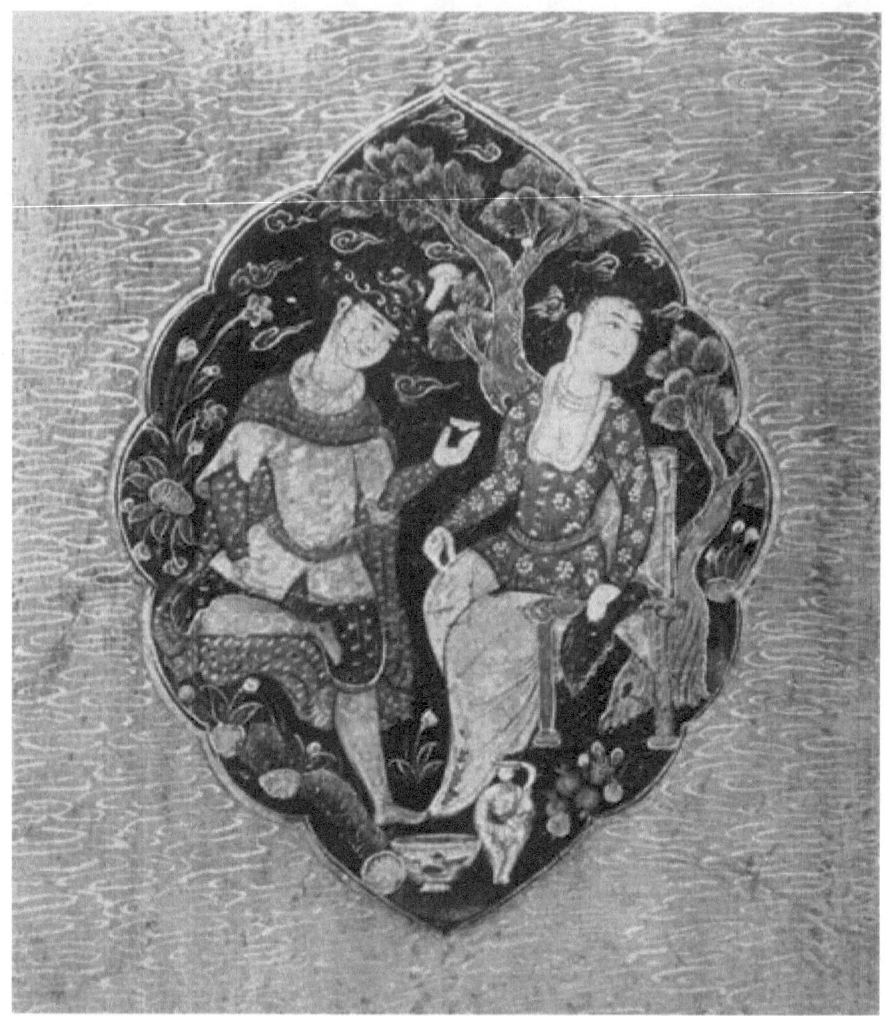

RIZA ABBASI, FAVORED COURT ARTIST, PORTRAYS EUROPE-ANS AT THE COURT OF SHAH ABBAS THE GREAT (A.D. 1588-1629)

Detail of exquisitely painted woodwork from the Pavilion of CHAHAL SITUN (Hall of Forty Pillars), the Palace at Ispahan built by SHAH ABBAS.

The young Shah, who was pleased with the leader of the party (Europeans), gave him royal gifts, Sir Anthony Sherley records (1598), including "forty horses all furnished, two with exceeding rich saddles, plated with gold, and set with rubies and turquoises." To these he added camels, tents, and a sum of money.

The fusion of MUHAMMADAN doctrine with this Aryan (Persian) culture of old,[8]

[8] "PERSIAN influence increased at the court of the CALIPHS, and reached its zenith under AL-HADI, HARUNU'R-RASHID, and AL-MAMUN. Most of the ministers of the last were PERSIANS or of PERSIAN extraction. In BAGHDAD, PERSIAN fashions continued to enjoy an in-

is an important event in the history of Art. For out of this fusion came forth into being a new phase of artistic expression completely different, in form and spirit, from its predecessors. Probably of equal importance is the fact that, although practised by divers races and subjected to many developments, fluctuations and variations, it has retained throughout the centuries its identical characteristics. What was the vital force that brought about this cultural evolution and unification? The answer appears to be RELIGION, as we shall see.

The foundation of the MUHAMMADAN EMPIRE was RELIGION. It was to the Holy Standard that the nations bent and professed unqualified allegiance. A powerful political unity came into existence and continued for a period of SIX centuries uninterrupted. The nations of this united kingdom of ISLAM were thus merged into one unit, under the stimulus of one formal religion, freely transmigrating local ideas. Arts and culture were transformed, but the evolution thus caused by the Religion was essentially political in nature.

> *"Lips sweet as sugar on my pen bestow,*
> *And from my book let streams of odour flow."*

—J'AMI.

ILLUSTRATED AND ILLUMINATED MANUSCRIPT

The complete volume of "YUSUF-OU-ZALIKHA", the popular poem by the famous mystic poet J'AMI, based on the Biblical story of JOSEPH and POTIPHAR'S WIFE. The scribe, MIR ALI SULTANI.

The colophon reads:

"Terminated by the sinner, humble MIR ALI SULTANI the penman, may God forgive his sins and shelter his faults. Terminated in the month of MOHARRAM AL HARAM in the year A.H. 944 (in letters) (A.D. 1537) in the glorious city of BUKHARA."

The Dedication in the handwriting of the scribe, in ornate gold lettering, reads:

"For his majesty, the AUGUST, the just, the possessor of virtues, the great KHA-GAN GHAZI ABD-UL-AZIZ BAHADUR KHAN, may his domain last forever."

The autograph of the Emperor SHAH JAHAN, the "GREAT MOGUL", on the magnificently decorated mount reads:

"In the name of God compassionate and merciful this YUSUF-OU-ZALIKHA treasured on the occasion of BLESSED ACCESSION." (A.D. 1627)

In confirmation of the foregoing, it is of great interest that JAHANGIR makes special reference in his memoirs (Tuzuk-i-Jahangiri) to an incident, as of highest importance, that he was presented by ABD-AL-RAHIM KHAN, KHAN-I-KHANAN, with

creasing ascendancy. The old PERSIAN festivals of the NAWRUZ, MIHRGAN, and RAM were celebrated. PERSIAN raiment was the official court dress, and the tall, black, conical PERSIAN hats were already prescribed as official by the second ABBASID Caliph (in A.H. 153: A.D. 770). At the court the customs of the SASSANIAN Kings were imitated, and garments decorated with golden inscriptions were introduced, which it was the exclusive privilege of the ruler to bestow. A coin of the Caliph AL-MUTAWAKKIL shows us this Prince actually clothed in true PERSIAN fashions".—VON KREMER, Streitzuge, page 32.

a superb copy of J'Ami's poem Yusuf-ou-Zalikha, transcribed by Mir Ali Sultani, "Prince of Penmen", and that the gift was appraised at "a thousand Muhr".

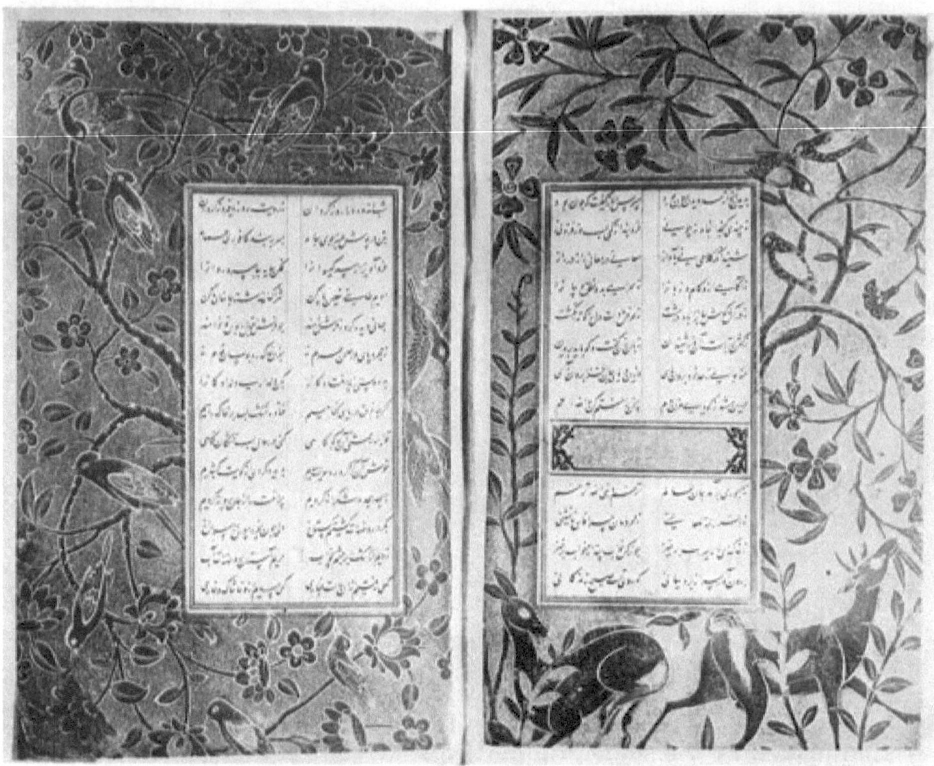

COMPLETE ILLUSTRATED AND ILLUMINATED MANUSCRIPT OF "YUSUF-OU-ZALIKHA", BY THE FAMOUS MYSTIC POET J'AMI

ONE OF THE ILLUSTRATIONS TO THE MANUSCRIPT YUSUF-OU-ZALIKHA

Zalikha in old age, broken and in poverty, meets Yusuf in the market place in Egypt.

"Where is thy youth, and thy beauty, and pride?"
"Gone, since I parted from thee," she replied.
"Where is the light of thine eye?" said he.
"Drowned in blood-tears for the loss of thee."
"Why is that cypress tree bowed and bent?"
"By absence from thee and my long lament."
"Where is thy pearl, and thy silver and gold,
And the diadem bright on thy head of old?"...

—Quotation from Yusuf-ou-Zalikha (J'Ami).

Translation of R.T. Griffith.

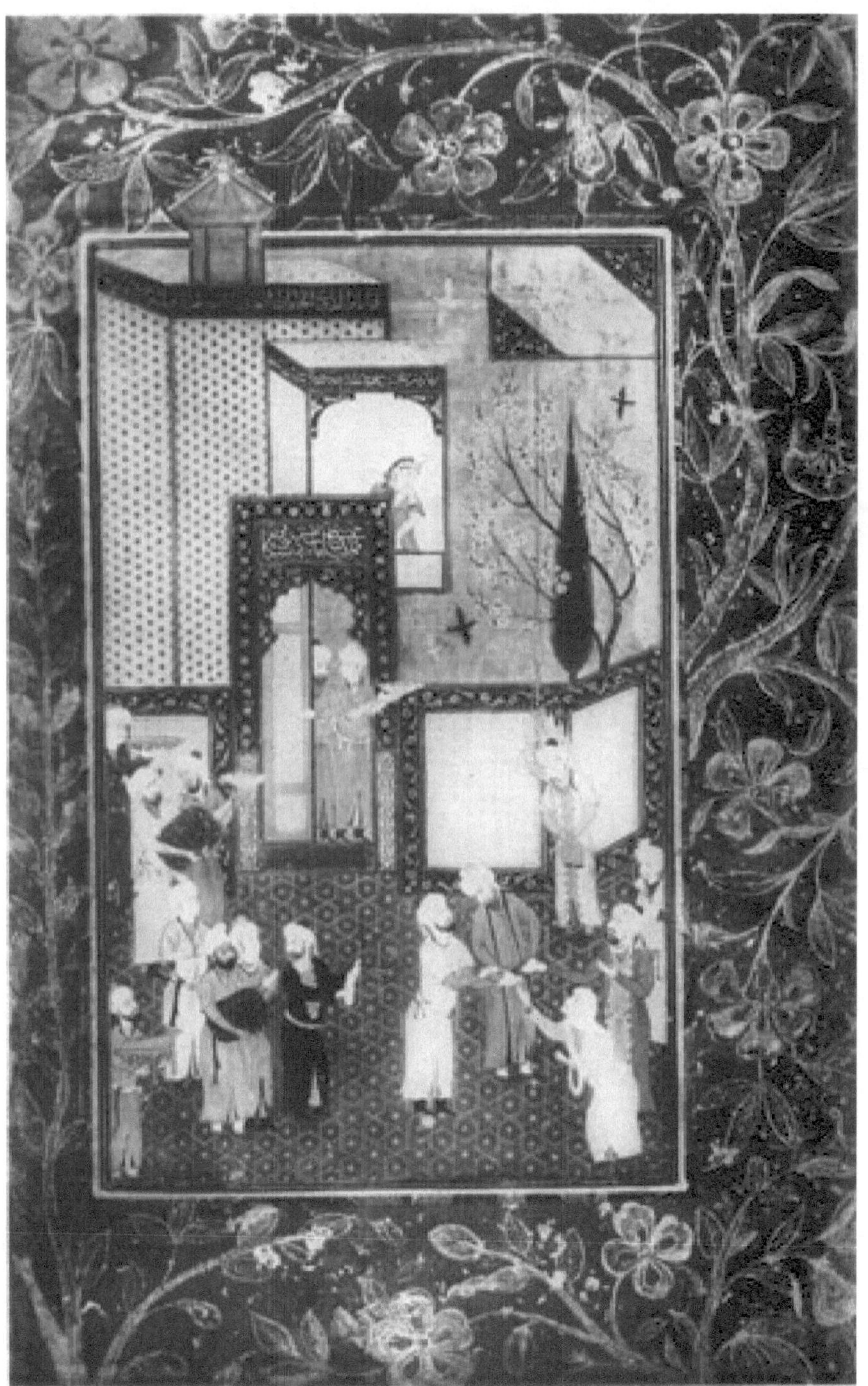

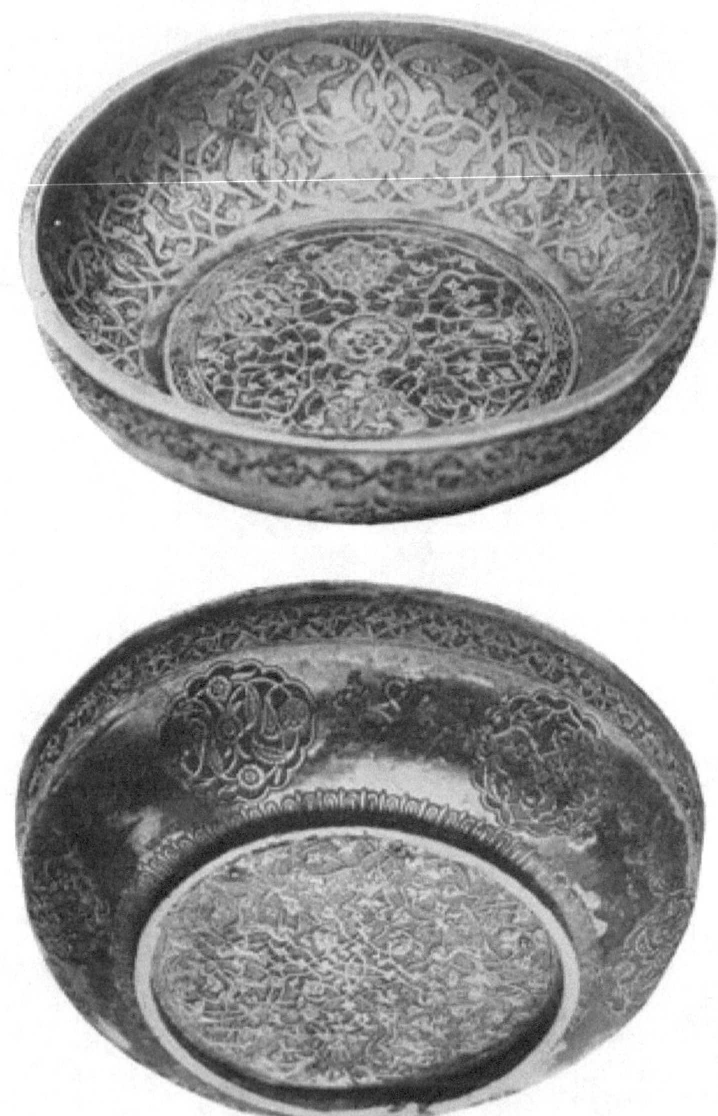

CHISELLED SILVER BOWL, DECORATED IN FILIGREE AND POLYCHROME ENAMEL. PERSIAN WORK OF THE XVITH CENTURY, PROBABLY EXECUTED IN ASIA MINOR FOR A PRINCELY OTTOMAN PATRON

"There is no God but God," said the Apostle of Arabia, but the poet reflected awhile, and his rejoinder was: "The Ways of God are as the number of souls of men."

The Prophet's religion was rational, its principles attainable; it secured for the poet social amelioration and physical comfort, but there was a voice from the depth of his soul that he could not silence. It was the voice of mystery; he was concerned with the problems of the "Wherefore, the Whence, and the Whither"…. Was he not a Son of the land which PLOTINUS visited to learn mystery of the Orient of Old?[9]

We have to look therefore to the RELIGION, "The Ways" of whose God "are as the number of Souls of Men", to perceive the true nature of the evolution of the artistic expression of these people.

Souls with irresistible cravings for Mysticism, poets, artists, philosophers and the like, discovered for the first time from MUHAMMAD's formal teachings, which contained certain esoteric elements, that the senses, unreal and phenomenal, have yet an important mission to fulfill in the task which aims to escape from SELF (which is an illusion and the root of SIN, PAIN, and SORROW) and to attain the height where the eternal beauty, which is but ONE, reveals itself through countless phenomena which are but reflections of ONE. "The PHANTASMAL is the BRIDGE to the REAL," says the mystic, and the immortal lines of J'AMI read:

> *"Though in this world a hundred tasks thou tryest,*
> *'Tis Love alone which from thyself will save thee.*
> *Even from earthly love thy face avert not,*
> *Since to the real it may serve to raise thee.*
> *Ere A, B, C, are rightly apprehended,*
> *How canst thou con the pages of the* QUR'AN?
> *A sage (so heard I) unto whom a scholar*
> *Came craving counsel on the course before him,*
> *Said, 'If thy steps be strangers to love's pathways,*
> *Depart, learn Love, and then return before me,*
> *For, shouldst thou fear to drink wine from form's Flagon,*
> *Thou canst not drain the draughts of the Ideal.*
> *But yet beware, Be not by form belated,*
> *Strive rather with all speed the bridge to traverse.*
> *If to the bourn thou fain wouldst bear thy baggage,*
> *Upon the bridge let not thy footsteps linger."*[10]

"PORTRAIT OF MEHDI ALI GULI KHAN, COMMANDER OF FORTRESS, BY RAMDAS"—A.D. 1630.

A leaf from the National Portrait Album conceived by the Emperor AKBAR, and amplified and executed by JAHANGIR and SHAH JAHAN. The volume consists of portraits of the Royal Family of the GREAT MOGULS and their principal supporters.

[9] "Il prit un si grand goût pour la philosophie qu'il se proposa d'étudier celle qui était enseignée chez les Perses et celle qui prévalait chez les Indiens. Lorsque l'empéreur Gordien se prépara à faire son expédition contre les Perses, Plotin, alors âgé de trente-neuf ans, se mit à la suite de l'armée. Il avait passé dix années entières près d'Ammonius. Gordien ayant été tué en Mesopotamie, Plotin eût assez de peine à se sauver à Antioche." —PORPHYRY ON PLOTINUS: Translation of the Enneads of Plotinus (Bouillet; Paris, 1857).

[10] "Religious Systems of the World" (Swan Sonnenschein, 1892).

These historic personages are represented in the centre as single individuals, with their chief officials and retainers in the border around them.

RAMDAS, a Hindu artist, was one of AKBAR's artists who worked under JAHANGIR and SHAH JAHAN. His signed works include the following:

BABURNAMA in the British Museum and South Kensington Museum.
AKBARNAMA in South Kensington Museum.
RAZMNAMA in the State Library, Jaipur, India.
TIMURNAMA in the Oriental Public Library, Bankipur, India.

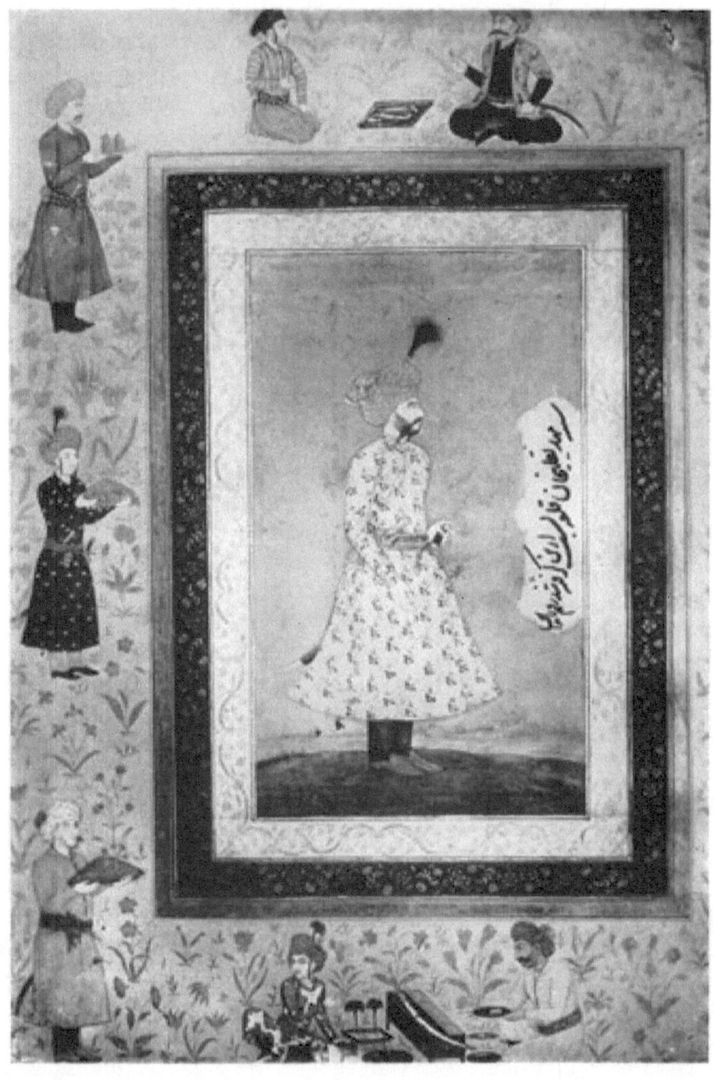

"PORTRAIT OF MEHDI ALI GULI KHAN, COMMANDER OF FORTRESS, BY RAMDAS"—A.D. 1630

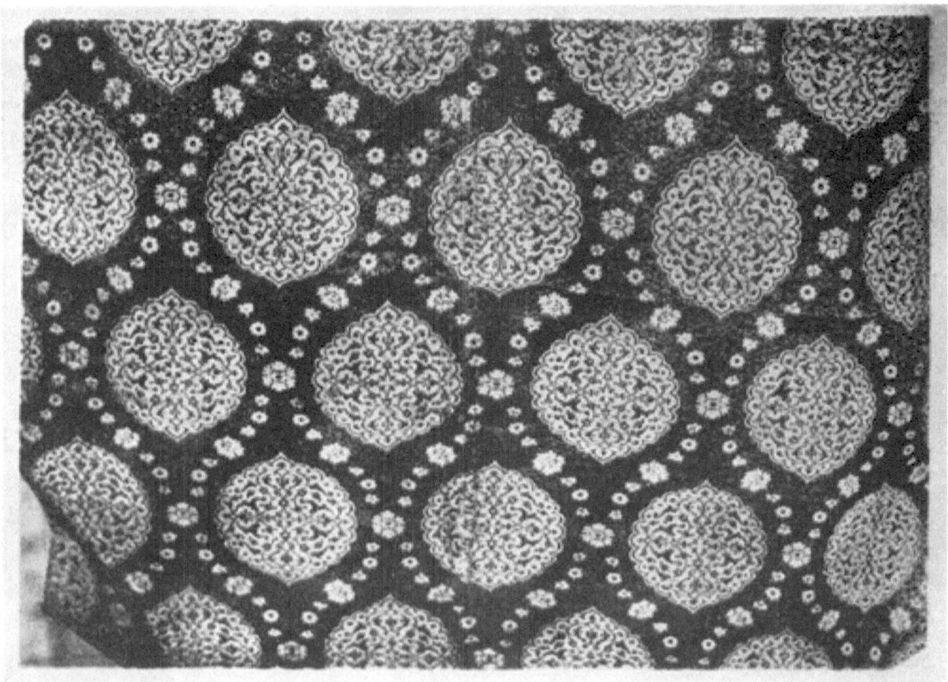

SILK FABRIC—A RARE EXAMPLE OF THE KIND PRODUCED BY THE ROYAL LOOMS AT ISPAHAN, WHICH FLOURISHED UNDER THE DIRECT PATRONAGE OF SHAH ABBAS THE GREAT (A.D. 1588-1629)

"Oct. 18th, 1666.—To Court. It being ye first time his Maty (CHARLES II of England) put himself solemnly into Eastern fashion of vest, changeing doublet, stiff collar, bands and cloake, into a comley dress, after ye Persian mode. I had sometime before presented an invective against our so much affecting the French fashion, to his Majesty, in which I took occasion to describe the comelinesse and usefulness of the Persian clothing, in ye very same manner his Maty now clad himself."—JOHN EVELYN (A.D. 1666), celebrated historian and diarist.

The unreality of things material, the illusion of Self and desires, the perception that all living things and apparent phenomena reflected but one all-embracing GOOD and BEAUTY, was the philosophy of Hindu and all Oriental mystics of old; but they attempted to destroy the self and desires (Source of Sin) uncompromisingly and unreasonably. It was a philosophy "cold" and "bloodless", as Professor BROWNE points out, in trenchant terms. The MUHAMMADAN mystic became conscious that the stream cannot be crossed without the aid of the BRIDGE constructed for this purpose.

Here (as it seems to us) lies the KEYNOTE, the mainspring of inspiration of artistic expression, which (for the lack of better designation) might be termed MU-HAMMADAN ART: A merging of physical and spiritual, of worldly magnificence and eternal bliss.

THE PRINCES OF THE HOUSE OF TIMUR

EMIR TIMUR (TIMUR-I-LANG) on the throne (A.D. 1335-1405)

On the right of the throne:

 BABUR A.D. 1526-1530
 HUMAYUN A.D. 1530-1556
 AKBAR A.D. 1556-1605
 JAHANGIR A.D. 1605-1627
 SHAH JAHAN A.D. 1627-1658

On the left are three sons of SHAH JAHAN:

 DARA SHIKOH
 SHAH SHUJA
 AURENGZIB
 (who succeeded Shah Jahan)

 MUGHAL Painting from the Imperial Library of DELHI, A.D. 1640

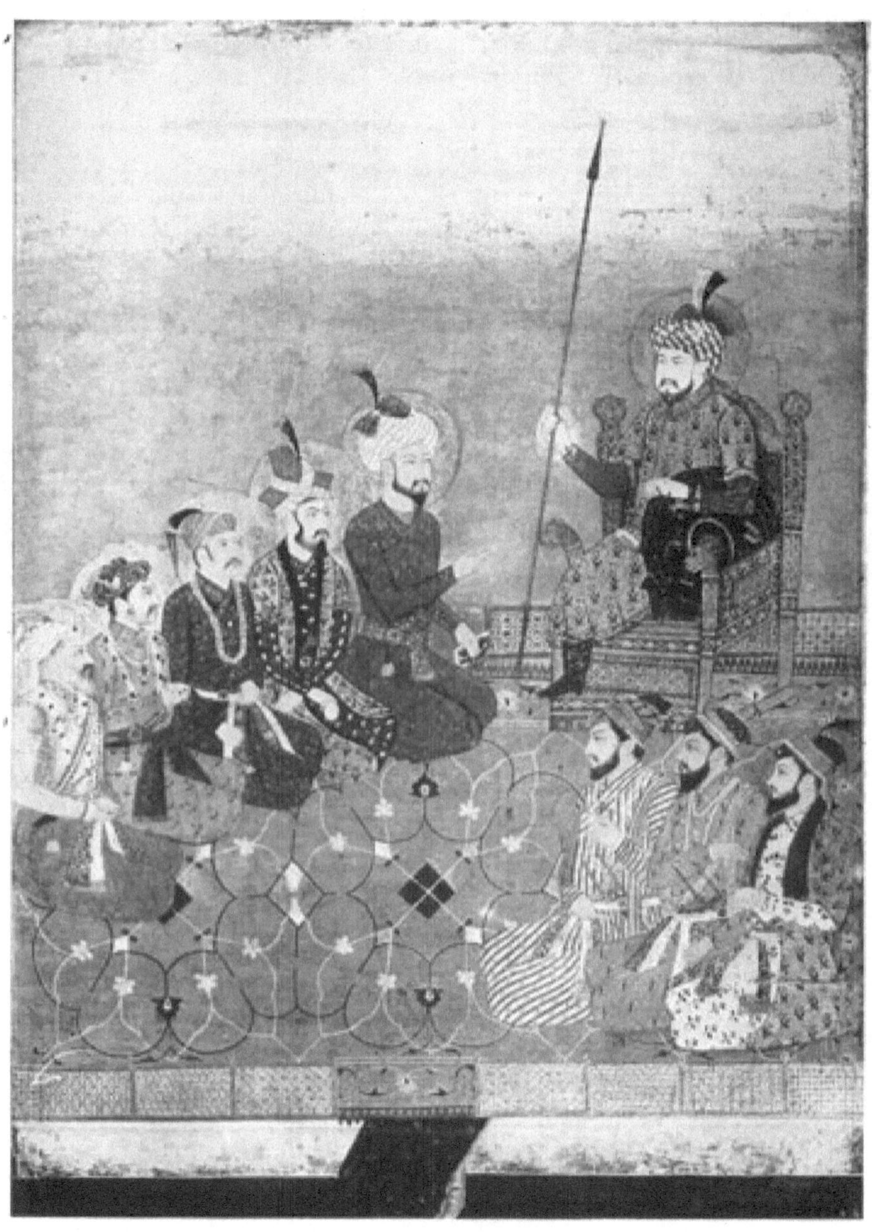

THE PRINCES OF THE HOUSE OF TIMUR
MUGHAL PAINTING FROM THE IMPERIAL LIBRARY OF DELHI,
A.D. 1640

TALAR (HALL OF AUDIENCE) RUG

From the looms of ISPAHAN or the adjoining city of JOSHAGAN. Made during the reign of SHAH SULEIMAN (A.D. 1667-1694), upon the model of CHAHAR BAGH Royal Garden at ISPAHAN, on the grounds of which the Royal Pavilion of HASHT BAHISHT (Eight Paradises) stands. The Rug measures 29 feet by 9 feet 5 inches.

LORD CURZON in his History of Persia, Vol. II, page 38, gives the following description of the Garden of CHAHAR BAGH:

"At the upper extremity a two storeyed PAVILION connected by a corridor with the SERAGLIO of the palace, so as to enable the ladies of the harem to gaze unobserved upon the merry scene below, looked out upon the centre of the avenue. Water conducted in stone channels ran down the centre, falling in cascades from terrace to terrace, and was occasionally collected in great square or octagonal basins where cross roads cut the avenues. On either side of the central channel was a row of chenars and a paved pathway for pedestrians, then occurred a succession of open parterres, usually planted or sown. Next on either side was a second row of chenars, between which and flanking walls was a raised causeway for horsemen. At intervals corresponding with the successive terraces and basins, arched doorways with recessed open chambers overhead conducted through these walls into the various royal or noble gardens that stretched on either side and were known as the gardens of the throne; nightingale, vines, mulberries, Dervishes, etc. Some of these pavilions were places of public resort and were used as coffee houses, where when the business of the day was over the good burghers of Ispahan assembled to sip that beverage and inhale their Kalians the while. At the bottom quays lined the banks of the river and were bordered with the mansions of the nobility."

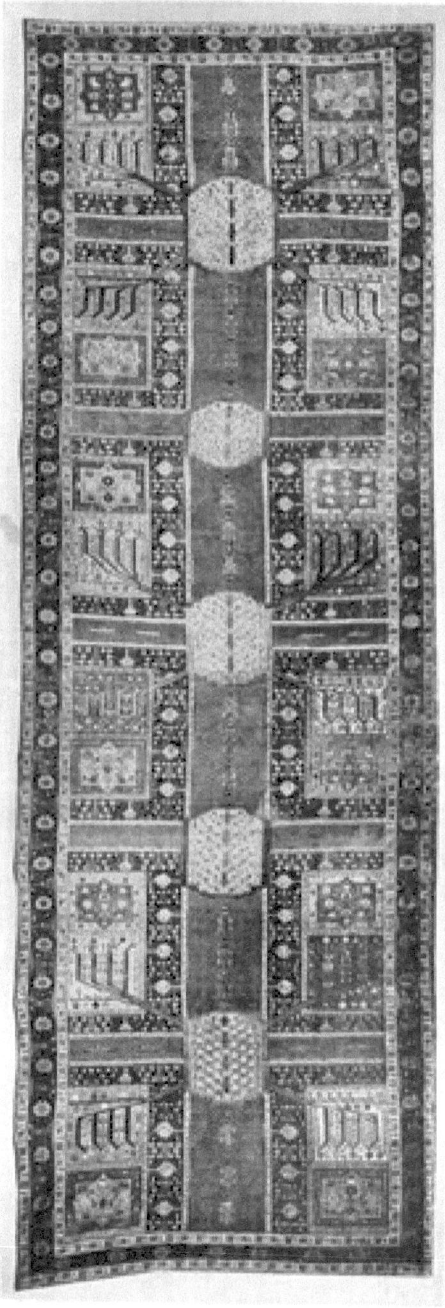

A desire to reach to our higher instincts through the vehicle of our senses is
apparent in all forms in which these masters sought to express themselves; we feel
that, in their entrancing rhythmical compositions, in their incomparable poetry of
flowing melodious words, in all their literature, in the inimitable colors and lyrical

lines of all branches of representation of visual art. We feel the presence of an element prevailing throughout, and underlying every form of expression, an element which may be described in a word, "HUMAN".

It is stated that the PERSIAN spirit and feeling were reflected in all forms of artistic expression of the MUHAMMADAN world. It is not, however, intended that other nations and countries over which ISLAM held sway, contributed nothing in the building of the influences of each were felt in varying degrees in the transmigration of ideas continued to take place between the nations, and the influences of each were felt in varying degrees in the transformation that resulted. In the fusion referred to, the influence of the PERSIAN culture was predominant, a fact so transparent, as to require (we may assume) no emphasis.

It is not intended to deal here with particular aspects or divers branches of arts in which the genius of these artists found expression. In offering briefly these lines as to the general aspect of the Art of the MUHAMMADAN world, the intention is to offer an explanation to those who may not be familiar with its history.

H. KEVORKIAN

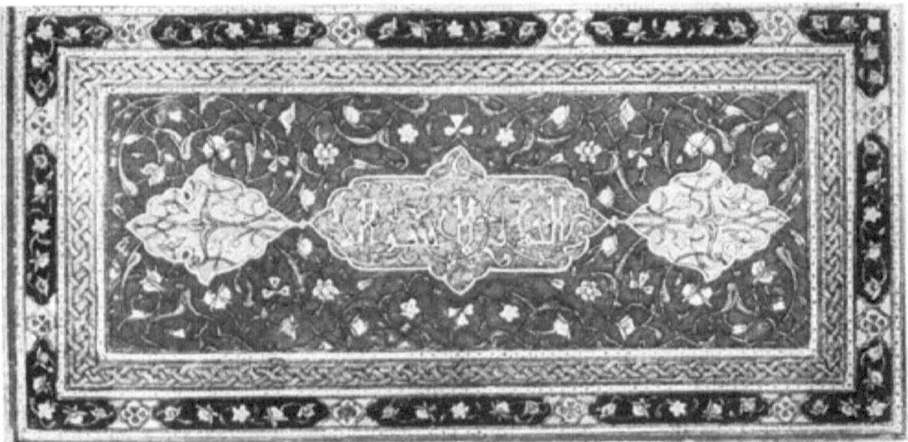

Lector House believes that a society develops through a two-fold approach of continuous learning and adaptation, which is derived from the study of classic literary works spread across the historic timeline of literature records. Therefore, we aim at reviving, repairing and redeveloping all those inaccessible or damaged but historically as well as culturally important literature across subjects so that the future generations may have an opportunity to study and learn from past works to embark upon a journey of creating a better future.

This book is a result of an effort made by Lector House towards making a contribution to the preservation and repair of original ancient works which might hold historical significance to the approach of continuous learning across subjects.

HAPPY READING & LEARNING!

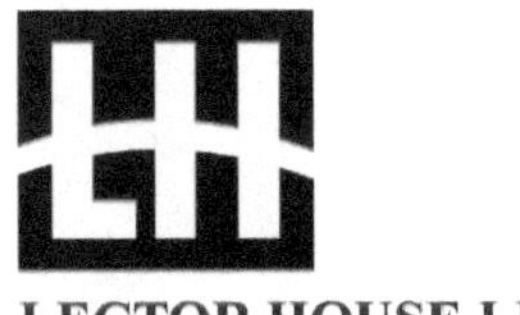

LECTOR HOUSE LLP
E-MAIL: lectorpublishing@gmail.com

www.ingramcontent.com/pod-product-compliance
Lightning Source LLC
LaVergne TN
LVHW091149180726
843490LV00004B/1388